I0088485

Weddings and Funerals
in the Church Building

Compiled By

Ron Halbrook and Mike Willis

Truth
Publications

Taking His hand,
Helping each other home.
TM

ISBN 10: 1-58427-170-1

ISBN 13: 978-158427-170-3

First Printing: 2006

Truth Publications, Inc.
CEI Bookstore
220 S. Marion St., Athens, AL 35611
855-492-6657
sales@truthpublications.com
www.truthbooks.com

Table of Contents

Why This Material?

From time to time, brethren come into the bookstore looking for material which addresses the subject of whether or not it is scriptural to have weddings and funerals in a church building. As a result of these requests, I asked Ron Halbrook to help me pull together some materials on this subject. Using his files, we were able to bring together this collection of material.

Neither of us is trying to push an agenda. We are not trying to campaign to get others to have or not to have weddings and funerals in the church building. In my own family both my son and daughter were married in ceremonies conducted in a location other than a church building; in Ron's family only one of his children has married at the time this is composed and it was not conducted in a church building. Nevertheless, both of us have conducted several weddings in church buildings and do not believe that the choice to have a wedding in the church building is a sinful choice. We both have preached at funerals which were conducted in church buildings.

Brethren generally have left this issue to the determination of each individual and each congregation. That is the proper and wise course. Brethren who approve funerals and weddings in church buildings are not liberals and brethren who have scruples are not fanatics or factionalists. Such differences should be discussed with mutual respect, patience, and forbearance within the bonds of love (Eph. 4:1-3). We all share the same fundamental commitment to Bible authority and to the spiritual nature and mission of the church.

The exchange between Ralph Williams and Weldon Warnock was a publicly produced written exchange whereas the exchanges between Ron and various friends were private, but both of them provide opportunities for both sides to be heard. The materials by Irven Lee, Herschel Patton, and Bill Cavender contain the publicly expressed judgments of seasoned gospel preachers who have not created division over these issues. They deserve to be read. We commend this material for your study.

Mike Willis

Funerals and Gospel Preaching

Ron Halbrook

The habits and customs associated with burying the dead vary from culture to culture and country to country. The range of differences includes superstitious rites and drunken feasts—everything on the spectrum from serious and pious to silly and pernicious. We live in a culture which permits, but does not dictate, funerals centered around devotion to God—prayers, sacred songs, and Bible teaching. Christians and gospel preachers should not hesitate or be ashamed to use this wonderful opportunity for proclaiming the gospel of Christ in its purity and simplicity.

The use of such a format is not specified in Scripture, but is authorized by every passage that mandates gospel preaching, beginning with Matthew 28:18-20 and on down the line. The habits of a culture and the setting of a society modify the format of opportunities for preaching Christ. But the context of the gospel is settled in the heavens and not subject to change. The facts, commands, and promises of the gospel are the same for every culture and society—for all men!

> For I delivered unto you first of all that which I also received, how that Christ died for our sins according to the scriptures; And that he was buried, and that he rose again the third day according to scriptures (1 Cor. 15:3-4).

And he said unto them, Go ye into all the world, and
preach the gospel to every creature. He that believeth and
is baptized shall be saved; but he that believeth not shall
be damned (Mk. 16:15-16).

Opportunities which once existed in synagogues and
public forums for gospel preaching shifted in another
time and place to open fields, brush arbors, and school
houses—then to the town square—now to public media
like newspapers, radio, and television. Formal debates as
we know them involve unique features—such as bringing
false teachers into meeting houses built for preaching the
truth. No principle is violated; it is a format for accom-
plishing the victory of truth and the harvest of souls. The
Bible authorizes gospel preaching—even debates with
formal propositions, moderators, bed-sheet charts, over-
head transparencies, and the like—but does not specify
those details. If the habits and customs of a people open
the door to gospel preaching on the occasion of a wedding, a baby's birth, or the solemn burial of the dead, we
are authorized to utilize that door.

Some brethren have scruples and would agree we can
use the funeral opportunity for gospel preaching only if
we do so outside of, and away from, the meeting house.
"That is to be used only for the Lord's work." Yes, and
what is gospel preaching if it is not the Lord's work? We
can go to where the people are to do this work, as Paul
"preached Christ in synagogues" (Acts 9:20). Or, we can
open our meetings to "those that are . . . .unbelievers" so
that they can come to where we are (1 Cor. 14:23). And it
does not change the case whether we meet under a tree, in
the personal dwelling place of a member, or in a meeting
house built "for the Lord's work."

If a people had the habit of calling upon God for guidance when a new baby entered the family, we could go to a family or invite the family into our meeting house in order to preach Christ to them. This has nothing to do with infant baptism or infant membership in the church, and is used merely to illustrate. Whether the family brought the baby in arms or not, would not change the case—whether the couple to be married "dressed up" for the occasion or not, would not change the case—whether the grieving people brought the casket with the dead in it, with or without flowers on the casket, would not change the case. From the vantage point of God's people, the point and the purpose is to preach the gospel of Christ, to reach the lost, to do the Lord's work!

To use such occasions and formats for preaching God's word does not mean the church can build hospitals for babies to be born in, for engaged couples to obtain blood tests, or for dead people to be pronounced "dead." The church is not authorized to build court rooms and to pay the salaries of civil judges to settle the legal ramifications of birth, marriage, and death. There is no authority and this is no argument in favor of the church conducting day care centers, newly wed showers, or embalming services. We do have authority for local churches to use every possible format, arrangement, and opportunity for gospel preaching.

Brethren, let's not hesitate to preach the gospel of Christ, both in arrangements by which people come to us and in arrangements by which we go to them. Funerals open wide the door to preach the great themes of the gospel—the certainty of death, the sinfulness of sin, judgment to come, the universal need of a Savior, the terms of pardon, the resurrection, and the hope of heaven through the forgiveness in Christ Jesus! What we preach, not the place where we preach it, is the vital thing.

David Lipscomb (1831-1917) was asked about "Funeral Preaching" and responded in the *Gospel Advocate*, IX, 9 (28 Feb. 1867):173-74. In reprinting his article, we have italicized some of his words for emphasis. He beautifully painted the opportunities we may have in peaching Christ when death has come to someone's door. Let us be stirred to show genuine sympathy to our fellow man and to realize *the highest degree of kindness we can bestow upon him "is to teach him the truth, and to direct him to the path appointed and marked out by God, to lead mortals to heaven."*

Funeral Preaching
David Lipscomb

Brother Lipscomb: We hear very often, in this country, of our brethren preaching funerals. Now, when I joined the church it was the understanding that we were required to believe nothing but that which was taught plainly in the New Testament, nor require any thing else of others. I have searched diligently for command or example for it, and have failed to find any. I may be blinded. Will some brother who preaches funerals tell us the chapter and verse, that we may no longer grope in darkness?
Yours in the one hope,
J.M. Mulliniks

Response: We certainly find no authority for preaching funerals in the Bible. But we do find authority to preach the Gospel the word of life, in season and out of season, in other words, to be always ready *to preach the word of life to dying men.* The Christian must stand ever ready, watching and anxious whenever occasion offers to point his dying fellow creatures to the Lamb of God who taketh away the sin of the world, and to impress upon them a proper conception of the uncertainty and nothingness of life; of the certainty of death, judgment to come, and the awful weight and importance of eternity. This work can often be done effectually when death has come close to our own doors, snapt as under the tender tendrils of affection that entwine themselves around our own heart strings, and have taken from earth the dear idols of our hearts. In death, the death of a parent, brother, sister, child, or friend, God gives us *a lesson on these subjects of the uncertainty of all things earthly, the certainty of death, and of the necessity on the part of men to be prepared to pass the Jordan of death and enter the glorious home of the spirits of the just made perfect*, rather than to be consigned to the dark abodes of death, to the eternal companionship of the Devil and his furies.

God in death teaches this lesson, but man in his mad career after the mammon of this world, in his vain search after happiness in the gratification of his appetites and passions, fails to read the lessons. *Surely there is no harm, can be none, in the Christian man pointing him to this lesson*, and impressing it upon his heart, while it is softened by sorrow, and is opened, perhaps has been ruthlessly torn open by the unrelenting hand of death. The Christian may then "in season" improve the lesson of God's teaching, and pour into the torn and lacerated heart the healing oil of hope, that is found in a confiding trust in Jesus, the anointed Savior. But when men preach something else beside the Gospel, when they teach that salvation can be gained otherwise than through a full and an entire acceptance of Christ in a submission to all of his appointments, evil is done. That this is frequently done in the discourses preached at the death of individuals is true. It is equally true, that the same thing is done on divers other occasions. There is no more sin in making such an impression at the death of an individual than at other times. Such preaching is wrong, evil in its tendency and exceedingly sinful at funerals or any other times. The man that will cater to the prejudices and preach to please the friends of the deceased rather than to please God, will preach to please man rather than God at other times, and is unworthy to speak in the name of Christ.

The great need is, men who love the truth better than they love popular favor, who had rather please God than man; who feel that the highest degree of kindness they can bestow upon their fellow man, is to teach him the truth, and to direct him to the path appointed and marked out by God, to lead mortals to heaven. Such men will preach the truth on all occasions in the love of it. Such an one that has confidence and trust in God, and true Christian love for his fellow men, can preach without evil influence or sin in the presence of the living and the dead, at a birth or a death, and he will always honor God and benefit his fellow man in preaching. But when a man preaches anything else than Christ and Him crucified, than justification, through humbly following Christ in His appointments, walking in the ways He has marked out for us, that man does evil, and is guilty of cruelly leading men down to endless death. Such preachers, and such preaching, should be discountenanced. Such preachers are unworthy to preach at funerals or away from them. Men of faith, who love the truth; men of courage, who can tell the truth; men of devotion, who can suffer for the truth, are the great crying needs of the church and the world.

Guardian of Truth, XXVIII: 5 (March 1, 1984), pp. 139-140.

Exchange of Views on Funerals and Weddings in the Church Building

By Ron Halbrook and Several Friends
(Prepared 3-20-98)

(The following note and letter dated December 5, 1997 went to a number of friends who are brethren in Christ. This letter is the basis for the exchanges which follow. I removed some personal references unrelated to the subject at hand. **Ron Halbrook***)*

December 5, 1997th Year of Our Lord
Dear _____,

Thank you for your question asking about how we establish Bible authority for funerals and weddings in the church building. Back in the spring, I held a gospel meeting with the Knollwood church in Beavercreek, OH and preached one night on "Differences Not Requiring Division." I asked them to send you a copy of the tape because part of the sermon deals with your question. Perhaps you have received it. I'm enclosing several things from a file of information I've collected through the years on this subject, including three charts from the sermon.

Funerals and weddings can emphasize the secular or

the spiritual. It is not wrong to have a funeral or wedding which emphasizes the secular. Instrumental music may be used with secular songs, friends can get up and tell secular stories, and similar secular activities may be included. Some facility other than the church building should be used for such purely secular events.

All faithful brethren understand and agree that the church building may be used for various occasions of Bible teaching including Sunday services, Bible classes, debates, singing schools, gospel meetings, vacation Bible schools, teacher training programs, men's training classes, and other such occasions. All such occasions and opportunities are authorized, though not specified, because the church is "the pillar and ground of the truth" (1 Tim. 3:15). Funerals and weddings emphasizing the spiritual are centered on Bible teaching. When I preach such a funeral or wedding, I preach the very same truths I preach on other occasions in church buildings. Church buildings have been provided for occasions and opportunities to teach God's Word.

The presence of a body in a casket does not change the truth I preach at a funeral, but rather emphasizes that truth as I discuss the brevity of life, God's plan of redemption, the terms of pardon, the urgency of obeying God, and related spiritual themes. As the people wanting to marry stand before me, it does not change the truth of Bible teaching on marriage and related spiritual themes presented. Their presence under such circumstances only further emphasizes the truth preached. When they repeat the vows, they simply agree to obey what has been read from God's Word.

If the State is willing to accept something we do as sat-

isfying some legal requirement, that does not change the essential nature of what we are doing—teaching and emphasizing the truth of God's Word on marriage. The fact that the State accepts such an occasion as satisfying certain legal requirements of marriage does not change the truth we preach one iota. If the State wanted to give a credit in school toward graduation for students attending Bible classes at church, the fact that the Stated accepted such occasions as satisfying certain legal requirements would not change the truth taught in Bible classes one iota. If the city of Troas had had a curfew at 11:00 PM, but allowed an exception for religious services, the fact that Paul's preaching til midnight satisfied a legal requirement would not have necessitated moving the service to another building (whether or not the brethren owned a church building).

Notice that brethren have separated secular from spiritual activities by permitting preaching to be done on the occasions of funerals and weddings in the church building but not social meals and other purely social activities (showers, receptions, etc.). These are the activities which are parallel to ice cream socials. The church does not provide embalming equipment or kitchen facilities—purely secular or social things!

It seems to me brethren are stretching a point when they shift the argument from the essential nature of the occasion—Bible preaching—to such things as: (1) the presence of friends standing with the bride and groom (could friends walk down the aisle with a penitent saint coming forward to confess sin, to give emotional support?), (2) the presence of flowers (can flowers be present on other occasions—can scenes of water and flowers be painted on the baptistry wall—can we have flower designs on curtains and carpets in the church building?), (3) the presence of a casket (can a person sit at the front in a wheelchair or lie on a stretcher in the church building on other occasions?), and (4) someone throwing rice as the newlyweds leave (can children throw leaves on each other in the church yard—can people tells jokes and discuss sports while walking down the steps of the church building?).

I hope these few thoughts along with the other materials being sent will help in your study of this question. You are certainly free to share this letter and the other materials with other people who may be interested in studying this subject. May God bless your study of His Word. I commend you for your desire that we base all that we do on Bible authority. I hope we can see each other at some time in the future. You are always welcome here at our house. Give our love to your parents.

In Christian love,
Ron Halbrook

Exchange With First Friend

December 7, 1997
Ron,

Thanks for forwarding your message concerning weddings and funerals in the church building. It is well written, properly makes the distinction between the work of the church and things that, although innocent in themselves are simply not the work of the church, and constitutes an appeal to the authority of the Scriptures. I have no problem with funerals in the church building. I have for years been unconvinced that weddings in the building are scriptural, and I am still unconvinced. My view is that the essential purpose of the wedding is to satisfy a legal requirement in order for two people to be legally married. While it is necessary for the couple to satisfy this legal requirement, this is not the work of the church. The Bible teaching is incidental to the legal, not the legal incidental to the Bible teaching. I use these two questions to emphasize the point. If we had an assembly in which the songs were about marriage, the prayers were about marriage, and a preacher preached a sermon about marriage, but no one got married, would that be a wedding? Conversely, if two people stand before an authorized representative of the state and exchange vows, but there are no prayers, songs or sermon, would that be a wedding? If my understanding is correct, the purpose and essential feature of a wedding is to satisfy a legal requirement. Social and religious aspects are incidental to its primary purpose. Thus, by its nature it is not the work of the church. Please correct me if this is wrong. I appreciate your gentle approach and appeal to Scripture. I sincerely wish I could be convinced I am wrong on this subject. I hope I'm not just being stubborn.

Brotherly,
Signed

• • •

December 9, 1997
Dear _____,

Certainly, two people can meet the legal requirements of marriage without gospel preaching, in which case the legal requirement is *the* essential thing, and, obviously, in that case some place other than the church building should be used. But, when a person getting married wants the Word of God proclaimed, thus demonstrating that marriage is *far more* than a social or legal matter, the *essential* thing is God's Word and all other considerations pale—they can be nothing more than incidentals. The fact that the government will accept such an occasion as satisfying the legal requirement does not change the fact that our focus is on teaching that God and God's Word are supreme, absolute, and essential to the institution of marriage, standing above every social convention and every legal system. Such proclamation is in keeping with the purpose of a church building, regardless of incidental considerations.

As you know, those who oppose funerals in the church building say the customary and social factors are the essential consideration in a funeral. They might adapt your two questions by replacing legal requirements with customary and social requirements. But, when the gospel is proclaimed in its purity and simplicity by faithful men in a funeral, the *essential* thing is God's Word and all other considerations pale—they can be nothing more than incidentals. The fact that such an occasion satisfies certain customary and social expectations does not change the fact that our focus is on teaching that God and God's Word are supreme, absolute, and essential to an understanding of life, death, and eternity. Such proclamation is in keeping with the purpose of a church building, regardless of incidental considerations.

I appreciate your thoughts. I hope the holiday season will be safe and enjoyable for you and your loved ones.
In Christian love,
Ron

• • •

December 10, 1997
Ron,
Thanks for your good reply. I always appreciate your thoughtful work. The best I can do at this point is put myself as the weak brother in Romans 14. I'm not really

convinced, but I wouldn't want to debate it. At least that won't disrupt fellowship. Stay in touch. Happy holidays to you and yours.

Brotherly,
Signed

Exchange With Second Friend

December 11, 1998
Ron,

Thank you for your thoughts on funerals and weddings in buildings. While you have some good thoughts, I still have some doubts.

You said, "All faithful brethren understand and agree that the church building may be used for various occasions of Bible teaching including Sunday services, Bible classes, debates, singing schools, gospel meetings, vacation Bible schools, teacher training programs, men's training classes, and other such occasions." The purpose of all the events you have mentioned is to reach the lost and/or edify the saved. That is *not* why weddings are planned, although I agree it may be a result. Could a church advertise the use of its building for weddings (done in a spiritual way)? None of the occasions that you mentioned involves flower petals being dropped down the aisle, candles being brought in, a ring bearer and flower girl for everyone's amusement, etc. If the gospel being preached is all that is needed to justify the activity, where do we draw the line with other activities as long as the gospel is preached at some point in them?

Using the same reasoning that you gave for weddings and funerals in the building, could we not also justify using a church building for a political rally to promote someone running for a political office if we emphasized the godly stand that person took on moral issues (abortion, homosexuality, divorce, etc.)? Many lessons are needed on such topics, and what better opportunity to present one? Would there be anything wrong with such a political rally in a church building?

I'm sure you have dealt with such questions many times before and have a ready response. I was raised around weddings in church buildings (I have only attended one funeral in a church building), so I never questioned such a practice until more recent years. I cannot say that it is definitely wrong to do so, but I do have doubts about it. That is enough to make it wrong for me.

I ask my questions in all sincerity. I would love to believe beyond any doubt that there is nothing wrong with funerals and weddings in the building. I hope that you can help me by responding to my letter.
In him,
Signed

• • •

February 19, 1998
Dear _____,
Thanks for your kind and thoughtful response. I am so behind in my work that I am answering some e-mail from last December, as you can see. I have a preaching trip to the west coming up the first two weeks of March and then leave for five weeks in the Philippines on March 26. Please keep these efforts in your prayers.

For the most part, I believe the reaction among brethren

against funerals and weddings in the building is largely
an over-reaction to liberalism. Certainly, things could be
done in a funeral or wedding which would not be appro-
priate for the meeting house, but the same can be said of
any other format of teaching. Please consider these few
comments for further study:

1. The purpose of having a funeral or wedding in the
church building is precisely because this occasion provides
a format for teaching both saints and sinners the will of God
on marriage, divorce, and remarriage (along with all sorts
of related principles of truth: God's authority over all of human life, etc.). Different formats of teaching may arise out
of different occasions for teaching. For instance, because
schools are out in the summer, and we want to teach young
people (both saints and sinners) as much truth as possible,
we may arrange a Vacation Bible School.

2. You asked about the possibility of a church advertising a funeral or wedding. In the U.S. culture and context,
this occasion for teaching is designed primarily for the
family and friends of the ones getting married. Also, in our
context, so long as the speaker is a faithful Christian and
we have every assurance to believe the truth will be taught,
we leave it up to the families involved to arrange most of
the details. That simply reflects the fact again that different
formats of teaching may arise out of different occasions for
teaching. All the particulars of a given teaching arrangement do not have to be identical to all other teaching arrangements, in order for the truth to be proclaimed.

In other cultures, a funeral or wedding might generally have a broader appeal beyond the circle of immediate
family and friends, which might allow for a more general

announcement. By the way, in the case of funerals, we do make a more public announcement, no matter where it is to be held. These are simply cultural peculiarities.

3. Such things as flowers, etc. which you mentioned are purely cultural symbols and practices, which are not universal, just like the veil of 1 Corinthians 11. This involves no change in the work or worship of God's people.

4. If a nation had customs connected with political events (election, inauguration, etc.) which created opportunities for Bible preaching on God's rule over the universe, the differences between his kingdom and the kingdoms of men, etc., certainly the church building could be used for such teaching. I would be willing to preach such a sermon to the elected officials and other citizens of the community, both saints and sinners. There would be this difference: Such a sermon obviously could not and would not constitute an election or an inauguration, whereas the government accepts such a sermon on marriage as satisfying its legal needs in constituting a marriage (with the couple promising to do what the sermon sets forth). Since you mentioned political rallies, I will observe that such a sermon would not fit the nature of a political rally with its shouting, selling all sorts of things, debating many matters which are purely civil and political, organizing parties, taking up collections, compiling mailing lists, etc., etc.

Different cultures present different occasions and formats for teaching and preaching God's Word. So long as we are free to teach that Word without restriction or limitation, we may utilize such occasions and formats—both in and out of the church building.

May God bless you, your family, and your work. Come to see us when you can.

In Christian love,
Ron Halbrook

• • •

February 21, 1998
Ron,

Thanks for your response. I can't say anything about being behind with your mail. I need to get the bundle of mail out of my own box before criticizing someone else for the letter that is in theirs. (Grin.)

>1. The purpose of having a funeral or wedding in the church building is precisely because this occasion provides a format for teaching both saints and sinners the will of God on marriage, divorce, and remarriage (along with all sorts of related principles of truth: God's authority over all of human life, etc.).>

Come on, Ron, do you really believe that when a young couple decides to have their wedding in a church building that it is for the purpose of teaching others God's will on MDR? Even if it was their motive, they could accomplish this _any_ place they had the wedding. Everyone I know of who had a wedding in a church building simply did so because it was a large and nice place to have it inside.

You missed my point about advertising a funeral or wedding. I did not mean advertising when one is going to take place, but instead advertising for _other_ people to use our building for such to be done. Why not tell the courthouse to tell all applying for a wedding license that we will provide the building and preacher free of charge for their wedding? I'm sure that some would accept the offer, and teaching could be done, but I've never heard of such an offer.

>3. Such things as flowers, etc. which you mentioned are purely cultural symbols and practices, which are not universal, just like the veil of 1 Corinthians 11. This involves no change in the work or worship of God's people.>

Do not most people focus more on the flowers, flower girl, ring bearer, bridal party, etc. than they do on what is said during a wedding? If the wedding is being held to teach, should that not be the main focus? We both know that any teaching accomplished at a wedding takes a back seat to everything else involved. You have stated that the church building would not be a proper place for promoting a political candidate that followed God's law because of all the other related activities (shouting, selling, taking up collections, compiling mailing lists, etc.), so why make an exception for the activities at weddings? (By the way, they take up collections at weddings. Most people call them wedding gifts.) If we called the activities associated with political rallies "cultural symbols and practices," would that justify them?

May the Lord bless you on your trips.
In him,
Signed

• • •

February 24, 1998
Dear _____,
    The press of time limits me to a few brief thoughts—
too many other things are pressing. We can have a differ-

ent conscience on this matter and continue to maintain mutual love and respect, as I know we shall do.

Your Response: >Come on, Ron, do you really believe that when a young couple decides to have their wedding in a church building that it is for the purpose of teaching others God's will on MDR?<

My Comment: The flippant tone of this response shows you really do not understand the conscience that some brethren have in these matters. "Come on, Ron, do you really believe," implies I am saying one thing but believe in my heart something else. Perhaps your attitude will be different with time and reflection on passages like Romans 14 (where brethren are taught to recognize each other as equally honest, sincere, and conscientious). Do I really believe the primary purpose and focus on such occasions is the proclamation of God's Word? Yes, I really believe this because my wife and I were very focused on wanting the occasion of our marriage to provide an opportunity for the proclamation of God's Word _more than anything else_. Yes, that was truly our focus. Yes, we selected a preacher who was well known for preaching the truth, the whole truth, and nothing but the truth. He did not speak vague generalities or social niceties, but he proclaimed the truth in its original purity, simplicity, and power. Yes, that truth can be preached in other places, but also it can be preached in a building constructed for the very purpose of proclaiming God's Word at every opportunity. When I die, I want my funeral preached in the meetinghouse with the very same purpose and the very same kind of powerful gospel preaching. If someone else prefers to have his wedding and funeral somewhere else, he will have my full respect, love, and fellowship as being equally conscientious with myself.

Your Response: >Why not tell the courthouse to tell all applying for a wedding license that we will provide the building and preacher free of charge for their wedding?<

My Comment: First, we are already listed in the phone books, and our very presence in the community makes us available for anyone wishing to approach us for such purposes. I have received such contacts all through the years as it is. Second, when I am contacted about weddings, I inquire whether there has been a divorce, and if so, on what basis. If there is not a scriptural divorce permitting an innocent mate to marry a new mate, I explain there can be no wedding (Matt. 5:32; 19:9). I require private Bible studies with people who ask about weddings (without exception, including my own sister when she married), and we cover in detail what the Bible teaches and the principles which will be presented in the wedding. In a similar way, unless I already know the people so well that they know what to expect, when asked about conducting a funeral, I make it plain that my funeral sermons are Bible centered, not social centered. The preaching I do at funerals and weddings is filled with Scripture, lasting 30-45 minutes, and includes the plan of salvation. People have been converted as a result of such occasions and I will continue to utilize such opportunities whenever possible. People seeking true Bible preaching on such occasions find faithful preachers to do it, but advertising to the general public would be an exercise in futility, frustration, and wasted time both for the general public and for myself. The general public does not want to hear the kind of preaching I do on such occasions. _____, if you heard what I and other faithful men preach on such occasions, you would know you had been to hear Bible preaching and not to be entertained at some social or secular function. I hope you will reflect on these comments with soberness of mind and not dismiss them with, "Come on, Ron, do you really believe. . . ?" We may not have the same conscience on this matter, but I am as ready to answer to God for my conscience on it as you are for yours. That does not prove either of us right, but it does remind each of us to regard the other as serious, sober, and sincere in conscience.

Your Response: >Do not most people focus more on the flowers, flower girl, ring bearer, bridal party, etc. than they do on what is said during a wedding? If the wedding is being held to teach, should that not be the main focus? We both know that any teaching accomplished at a wedding takes a back seat to everything else involved. You have stated that the church building would not be a proper place for promoting a political candidate that followed God's law because of all the other related activities (shouting, selling, taking up collections, compiling mailing lists, etc.), so why make an exception for the activities at weddings? (BTW, they take up collections at weddings. Most people call them wedding gifts.). If we called the activities associated with political rallies "cultural symbols and practices," would that justify them?>

My Comment: I don't know what "most" people focus on in any service—whether a typical Lord's day service, a funeral, or a wedding—but I always preach the truth to the best of my ability, taking into account who is in the audience and what their needs might be on each occasion. I have never focused more on the things you mentioned. A woman is more likely to comment on such things as flowers on any occasion, which is in keeping with her feminine nature and does not necessarily mean she fails to focus on the truth taught.

I could assert as easily as you do, "We both know that any teaching accomplished at a typical Lord's day assembly takes back seat to everything else involved—the preacher's tie, the ladies dresses, the color of the carpet, the color of the curtains, the cute young man serving at the table, how much time the service takes, how educated or eloquent the speaker is, etc." Are such things noticed and do people comment on them? Yes, but God did not ordain us to be judges of the hearts of men and to make a blanket statement that any teaching done takes back seat to these things. Someone might express such an opinion, but I intend to keep preaching God's Word with the confidence that it will fall into good and honest hearts.

I am amazed at your question, ". . .so why make an exception for the activities at weddings?" No exception is made, as is clearly evident from the illustration you yourself offer: the gifts. The gifts are given at the reception along with the meal and other social activities, all of which are held at some other location. This same clear line is seen in regard to funerals—after the preaching of God's Word, people go to some other facility for a meal and related social functions. Faithful brethren have recognized that distinction all through the years, just as they have recognized the difference between cultural symbols associated with any service in the meetinghouse and social activities conducted elsewhere.

Such statements as, "Come on, Ron, do you really believe. . . ?" and, "We both know. . . ," do nothing to sustain your arguments, but simply reflect that you do not regard brethren who have a different conscience from yours to be equally fair, honest, and sincere.

I am not offended at any of your thoughts and expressions, but simply want to caution you to drink deeply of the spirit which we are taught in Romans 14 on issues of this kind. May God bless you in your every effort to spread the gospel. Please keep me in your prayers.
In Christian love,
Ron

• • •

February 28, 1998
Ron,

I never meant to imply that *you* did not consider using a church building for weddings and funerals for the purpose of preaching the word. What I question is that reason being the reason for *most* who want to use a church building. I know of several who have had weddings in a church building, and all that I am aware of used the building for its appearance and size. Please forgive me if you felt that I was implying that was your reason also.

I admit, Ron, that I was unfairly judgmental in some of the things that I said, and I hope that you will forgive me for such. At the same time, I want to thank you for being straight with your responses, as I hoped you would be. I have often questioned the use of a church building for such occasions and have talked with several who defended it, but you have done the best job in removing any doubts that I may have. Some of your comments on funerals will help me with any I hold in the future, regardless of where they may be.

This subject is of immediate concern to me because I am presently scheduled to conduct a wedding in May, and right now a church building is the best place they have found to have it. Your comments have helped ease my mind and have helped me prepare for it.

Thanks again for your help, Ron.
In him,
Signed

• • •

March 14, 1998th Year of Our Lord
Dear _____,

I'm just back from my preaching trip out west. It went very well, by God's grace.

Thanks for your good post. I appreciate your openness to straightforward discussion. I am thankful to know you found our exchange helpful and you are not offended by it. Please be assured that when we engage in such discussions, I will not be offended. This exchange has been a blessing to me by forcing me to examine my position again in the light of Bible principles. I want to remain open to such study at all times. I know you feel the same way.

While I understand your concern that people not be overly focused on the size and appearance of the building, please consider two things. (1) Whatever building is used, it must accommodate the people who attend the funeral or wedding. That means that the size of the building is a legitimate concern. (2) The appearance is generally a concern to the ladies, much more so than to the men. This may reflect the natural inclination of females, who notice appearance about most things more than men, rather than reflecting secular impulses which are unhealthy. Whether or not funerals and weddings are held in a certain building, who usually has the best eye to select curtains, coordinate colors, etc. for the building: men or women? Certainly, concern for appearance can be overdone (and I make that point in a sermon I often use in gospel meetings), but, on balance, we need to factor in the reality that God did not make woman as a clone of man. He crafted and created a uniquely feminine nature, which we as men are sometimes slow to understand (1 Pet. 3:7).

I am glad to know you have accepted the opportunity to speak at an upcoming wedding, and wish I could be there to hear you. I am confident you will proclaim the truth of God's Word with love and boldness, without fear or favor. Remember that when you do so, God's Word does not return unto him void but accomplishes the purpose for which he sent it (Isa. 55:8-11).

Godspeed, my friend.

In Christian love,

Ron Halbrook

Exchange With Third Friend

December 13, 1997

Dear Ron,

After reading your letter, I had a couple of questions. I know, you are probably thinking, "What does this radical have to say about weddings and funerals in the building!" However, I will begin by saying that I don't mark brethren as liberal, nor "black ball" them in any way because they participate in this practice. With that being understood, I will say that I really question the activities. You made some very good points, but it all seems to boil down to one thing. Is it a religious activity or a secular activity. And, even if one desires to scramble the picture a little, is it a religious event with secular overtones, or a secular event with religious overtones. I think (for what that's worth!) that this question, and main point of alleged authority for the actions can be clarified in a couple of simple questions.

1. If these events are an evangelistic form of outreach as has been presented, then can the church collective pay for this endeavor, as they would for a gospel meeting, or other such evangelistically oriented actions. If not why not?

2. Is any music, vocal or otherwise allowed? I know you said no secular music. What about religious music? If so, is this performed by a chorus, or singers, not constituting singing "one to another"? If so, where is the Scripture that authorizes such a form of using the Lord's music for the purpose of one group of people singing to entertain another group of people who are not encouraged to sing back, and all of this during a supposed evangelistic endeavor of the church.

3. Is this activity under the oversight of the eldership? If so, in what way?

4. If this is a form of evangelism, would you be willing to put an ad in the paper that you will perform weddings and funerals for all comers at the Hebron Lane church of Christ? If not why not? What a spectacular idea for drawing folks from all walks of life, and from all over the city. You would have opportunity to preach to atheists, Jews, all denominations, etc.

These are just some late night thoughts, not meant to

be sarcastic in any way, but seeking to clarify the idea that these are secular, and not religious activities. I think question #1 will forever settle this. Then too, I have been wrong before, and will look intently at any response. However, at present, I see no way to get around this thought.

Thanks for your time,
Signed

P.S. One other quick thought after looking over your material again. You separate ice cream socials and eating from the marriage ceremony. Why? All are authorized activities, the only difference is that faithful brethren will hedge on one and not the other. Would it be wrong to have a potluck in the building if you were to preach a sermon on Matt. 6 while everyone was eating, thereby using the very occasion of God's good provision for us. I don't believe you can separate the two thoughts, just because one is fuzzy, and the other is a No-No.

• • •

February 22, 1998th Year of Our Lord
Dear _____,

I appreciate the good attitude expressed in your comments and, like yourself, I wish to keep my remarks on the highest plane of courtesy, dignity, and mutual respect. No, I don't consider anyone "radical" who is willing to discuss any Bible subject with such a demeanor. When we get beyond being questioned, we had better be infallible, but no one knows better than myself how very fallible I am. God's Word is the infallible standard by which we must test every matter of faith and practice. It is not a good sign when we get our hackles up because someone questions us. I am thankful for brethren who can discuss differences with a calm, cool disposition because this is a part of the learning and growing process for all of us.

Also, I appreciate your recognition that brethren can maintain mutual love and respect while having conscientious differences and personal scruples, and we may need time to work through certain subjects, without regarding each other as apostates. We must recognize both sides of the coin if our faith and life are to be balanced: *On the one hand*, we must "fight the good fight of faith," always contending earnestly "for the faith once delivered to the saints," in the face of clear digression and apostasy, just as you did in coming out of institutional liberalism (1 Tim. 6:12; Jude 3). *On the other hand*, we must patiently bear with each other in dealing with conscientious differences and personal scruples among brethren who are unreservedly committed to the truth (Eph. 4:1-3; Rom. 14).

Brethren who never learn how to deal with these matters "on the other hand," end up fussing, fighting, and fuming constantly—they frustrate themselves and everyone around them—they cause disruption everywhere they go—they float from place to place, leaving a wake of heartaches behind them, never settling down for very long anywhere, and consequently never really developing maturity or making a solid contribution to the cause of Christ. Furthermore, some churches with a conservative name get bogged down in internal strife over such matters and stifle the cause of Christ. Our forbearance is tested by dozens of such matters beside funerals and weddings in the building, and I once made a list of about 100 of them. Obviously, if we can't forbear with each other over such matters, brethren can't exist and function in a local church. We don't generally do much teaching about this problem, but I preached a lesson in my last meeting at Cob Hill on "Differences Not Requiring Division."

Now, I'll offer a few comments on your questions:

Your Question: "If these events are an evangelistic form of outreach as has been presented, then can the church collective pay for this endeavor, as they would for a gospel meeting, or other such evangelistically oriented actions. If not why not?"

My Answer: I'm not sure what you mean by "a form of evangelistic outreach." I'm most familiar with that expression from the denominations and liberal churches in a context where it means some so-called "ministry" (translate: social or recreational activity) which is used in effect to "bait" or entice people on one pretext when the goal is to somehow "slip in" some Bible teaching. For instance, a gym is justified as "a form of evangelistic outreach" on the basis that a brief devotional is held before or after games. Apparently, that is what you envision in regard to funerals and weddings in the church building because you spoke of "a religious event with secular overtones, or a secular event with religious overtones." That is light years away from what I presented. The funeral or wedding of which I speak is simply a Bible sermon focused on things associated with death or with marriage. Different occasions of teaching allow for different formats of teaching. Those who wish to have funerals and weddings not focused on Bible teaching need to have them elsewhere than the church building.

In the funerals and weddings with which I am familiar, the church is not directly involved beyond the fact that it permits individuals to use the building for an occasion of teaching God's Word. This is done on the basis that the building was built to expedite or provide for occasions of teaching God's Word in various formats. The church is involved to this necessary extent: We must be assured that sound, solid, scriptural teaching will be done. If necessary for some reason, an eldership could plan a funeral or wedding, and could invite as many or as few as they might deem expedient. In either case—whether individuals are permitted to make arrangements for such teaching or whether the elders were asked to do so—*the focus is on teaching God's word*. That is why the building exists. That is what makes it right.

You asked about the church paying for a funeral or wedding. There are no real expenses I am aware of—just open the doors and let the preacher preach. There are expenses for clothes, social get-togethers, etc., but they are incurred by individuals, just as is the case with any other occasion. When I want to get a new suit or have people over for refreshments after a gospel meeting, I don't ask the church to pay for such things.

Keep in mind the old baseball expression, *"Keep your eye on the ball."* I am discussing the church opening the doors for sound, solid, scriptural preaching and teaching—that is all. The presence of the dead person in a casket reminds us of our love for him and of the reality of death, but does not change one iota what is going to take place: *Sound, solid, scriptural preaching and teaching*— that is all. (By the way, I have preached such sermons on occasion when the body is not present for some reason— the preaching is still the very same.) The presence of the couple wanting to marry does not change one iota what is going to take place: *Sound, solid, scriptural preaching and teaching*—that is all. When I ask them whether they believe and will obey what is preached regarding marriage, that certainly does not change what we have done. The government recognizes our doing this for its own legal purpose, but that still does not change what we have done in proclaiming the truth of God's Word.

I will add this thought. Different occasions of teaching may have unique characteristics, but that does not change the essential nature of what we are doing. With funerals and weddings, the immediate family (and the persons wanting to marry) request we open the doors for the truth to be preached. This family and their friends are the ones most directly interested in this particular occasion of teaching. Therefore, we give them leeway in making some arrangements on an individual basis—within the limits of scriptural principles.

That thought leads me to another point that does not change the fact the church building is being used simply to teach the truth. The church itself may be the initiator of some occasion of teaching, or an individual (whether a local member or not) may be the initiator. For instance, a brother (local member or not) might ask us if he can use the building to get area song leaders together for some instruction and practice, perhaps because the acoustics of our building are excellent. Other than opening the doors or giving him the key to do so, we may not be directly involved—we would just give him the leeway to make the arrangements to use the building for this occasion of teaching on an individual basis. We would expect any expenses incurred for teaching materials to be borne by the individual making the request, and we would not expect to advertise it, but would allow the individual requesting the use of the building to decide whom to invite and how to do so. This arrangement would be unique to that occasion. Obviously, we would have the right to review each request by an individual for such use of the building to determine whether we thought the requested use would be within the limits of scriptural principles *and* whether we thought it would be expedient.

Your Question: " Is any music, vocal or otherwise allowed? I know you said no secular music. What about religious music? If so, is this performed by a chorus, or singers, not constituting singing 'one to another'? if so, where is the Scripture that authorizes such a form of using the Lord's music for the purpose of one group of people singing to entertain another group of people who are not encouraged to sing back, and all of this during a supposed evangelistic endeavor of the church."

My Answer: You asked whether the singing may be done by a group smaller than the whole assembly. If the church itself plans and provides an assembly, it would be my understanding that all need to sing, in keeping with the Ephesians 5:19 and Colossians 3:16, which require reciprocal action. If the church permits an individual to use the building for a teaching occasion, there could be more leeway in this sense: Passages such as James 5:13 show that individuals are authorized to sing religious songs outside the assembly conducted by the local church. They are not obligated to involve everyone present in the actual singing.

I believe small groups have been used at funerals out of fear that family and friends under the emotional pressure caused by the death of a loved one might not be able to sing effectively. Certainly, such singing was not done for entertainment (and no clapping, foot stomping, competition, or other things associated with entertainment were involved in any way). In the last 15-20 years, brethren have tried including everyone in the singing at funerals and have learned it generally works well. Nearly every funeral I've attended or had a part in during the last ten years has been conducted on this basis. A similar transition has gradually been occurring in weddings. My wife and I were married on Dec. 26, 1967 in the Pruett and Lobit Sts. Church of Christ in Baytown, TX. A couple of songs were sung by a small group before the service actually began, and then later, I believe near the close, everyone joined in singing "Blest Be the Tie That Binds." R.J. Stevens' songbook has some songs expressing what God teaches about the family, and these are being sung in the same way at more weddings now.

Your Question: "Is this activity under the oversight of the eldership? If so, in what way?"

My Answer: The use of the church building is under the oversight of elders. Under that oversight, elders may initiate and plan an occasion of Bible teaching, and they may permit individuals to plan some occasion of Bible teaching. Their oversight is maintained either way by the firm requirement that only _sound, solid, scriptural teaching and preaching_ be done.

Your Question: "If this is a form of evangelism, would you be willing to put an ad in the paper that you will perform weddings and funerals for all comers at the Hebron Lane church of Christ? If not why not? What a spectacular idea for drawing folks from all walks of life, and from all over the city. You would have opportunity to preach to atheists, Jews, all denominations, etc."

My Answer: You asked whether I would advertise in the paper, offering to preach on the occasions of funerals and weddings. I do not see a reason to do this, nor for the church to so advertise for the following reasons. First, we are already listed in the phone books, and our very presence in the community makes us available for anyone wishing to approach us for such purposes. I have received such contacts all through the years as it is. Second, when I am contacted about weddings, I inquire whether there has been a divorce, and if so, on what basis. If there is not a scriptural divorce permitting an innocent mate to marry a new mate, I explain there can be no wedding. I have private Bible studies with people who ask about weddings (without exception, including my own sister when she married), and we cover in detail what the Bible teaches and the principles which will be presented in the wedding. In a similar way, unless I already know the people so well that they know what to expect, when asked about conducting a funeral, I make it plain that my funeral sermons are Bible centered, not social centered. The preaching I do at funerals and weddings is filled with Scripture, lasting 30-45 minutes, and includes the plan of salvation. People have been converted as a result of such occasions.

People seeking true Bible preaching on such occasions find faithful preachers to do it, but advertising to the general public would be an exercise in futility, frustration, and wasted time both for the general public and for myself. The general public does not want to hear the kind of preaching I do on such occasions. If you heard what I and other faithful brethren preach on such occasions, you

would know you had been to hear Bible preaching and not
to be entertained at some social or secular function.

Your Question: "You separate ice cream socials and
eating from the marriage ceremony. Why? All are authorized activities, the only difference is that faithful brethren
will hedge on one and not the other. Would it be wrong to
have a potluck in the building if you were to preach a sermon on Matt. 6 while everyone was eating, thereby using
the very occasion of God's good provision for us. I don't
believe you can separate the two thoughts, just because
one is fuzzy, and the other is a No-No."

My Answer: On your added question, I would make
the same consistent separation which I have made in the
original letter: Separate the pot-luck from the preaching
and let the preaching be in the church building, just as the
preaching is in the building and the wedding reception is
elsewhere, just as the preaching is in the building and the
meal after the funeral is elsewhere.

Thanks for your patience with my rambling. Come to
see us when you can.
  In Christian love,
  Ron Halbrook

Exchange With Fourth Friend
December 7, 1997
Ron,
  I do have a question about weddings and funerals that
are conducted in facilities which are either rented or purchased and then maintained by the Lord's money. I would
love to be able to agree with you on this matter, but I need
some help on a point or two. You made the point that wed-

dings and funerals in the building are okay because of the
fact that during these events one gets to teach God's word
on vital subjects. I agree that funerals and weddings do
provide us with a wonderful opportunity to teach saints
and sinners and I try to take advantage of these opportunities when possible, but not in the church building. There
are several reasons for this but for now I would like to
share just a couple with you.

To be quite honest, I am afraid of an argument which
takes the thing which God has authorized ("teaching" in
this case) and turns it into the authority for another practice. Such reasoning would justify any practice as long as
the practice was legal and wholesome in and of itself. I do
not think it is sound reasoning to take that which is *authorized* and turn it into that which *authorizes*. When weddings and funerals are conducted in the church building,
why are people really there? Did they come to hear the
gospel and there *just happened* to be a dead man there?
Did they come to hear the gospel and two people *just happened* to be getting married at the same time? Wouldn't
this reasoning open the flood gates wide? Other social
practices could be authorized by simply teaching the Bible during the ceremony or practice.

The other problem I see with the practice is that the
argument that is used to defend it (opportunity to teach)
would demand that we have as many weddings and funerals in church facilities as possible! Since we all admit that
weddings and funerals are great opportunities to teach,
and since it is the church's duty to teach (1 Thess. 1:8),
one would be forced to say that churches should conduct
as many funerals and weddings as possible. One would be
forced to say that churches should advertise free use of the

building for these services in area newspapers and on the radio. We should do everything possible to encourage as many people as we could to have their weddings and funerals in the church building. Am I wrong in my conclusions?

Ron, I have not pressed my views on this matter and I don't intend to start now. But I would like for someone to help on my question about the nature of Bible authority. Church buildings are *only* authorized by the passages which tell us what we may do in them. (Right?) The only way (in my mind—which may well be wrong) to justify weddings and funerals in the building is to call them *lawful expedients* like song books and pews. But when one affirms such, he is forced to say that weddings and funerals in the church building facilitate in the accomplishment of God's will. Are we prepared for this conclusion? Is this a safe position to take? Let me know what you think.

Signed

• • •

December 9, 1997
Dear _____,

Thanks for your thoughts. On your first question (why does one thing [teaching] authorize another [funeral, wedding]), the funeral or wedding I'm discussing is simply another format for Bible teaching, just as a debate, Bible class, training class, or gospel meeting. It is not something *other than* teaching, but it *is teaching.* That is what makes it right to conduct it in the building. It would be wide of the mark to ask why "teaching" is used to authorize something else such as a debate, Bible class, training class, or gospel meeting. The authority for teaching is authority for various formats of teaching.

You asked why people come. Because they are invited by someone with whom they share confidence, friendship, or some relationship, just as occurs when most other teaching opportunities are created (gospel meeting, VBS, etc.). The very fact that the funeral or wedding is conducted in the church building conveys that it is a serious, sober, sacred matter to consider the meaning of such things as marriage, life, death, and eternity. If a person has any soberness about him at all, he comes fully expecting to hear words of truth and soberness from God's Word. I realize some denominational people might come expecting an entertainment extravaganza, but that is exactly what they would expect if they were attending a gospel meeting, VBS, or any other teaching opportunity. It is our job to present the truth so clearly and forcefully as to make the difference between true Bible preaching and entertainment-in-the-name-of-religion crystal clear.

You say, "Other social practices could be authorized by simply teaching the Bible during the ceremony or practice." It is not a matter of authorizing other *social* practices. The only "ceremony or practice" in this case is *Bible teaching*. Other occasions of *Bible teaching* are authorized by the same principle, not mere social practices. Notice, faithful brethren have always *separated* the social meals, parties, and showers from the occasion of the actual funeral or wedding, so that only Bible teaching is conducted in the meeting house. In a similar way, faithful brethren who want to have social gatherings before or after a gopsel meeting *separate* the social activities by conducting them in the family sphere before or after the preaching service, thus not in the church building.

On your second question, how many teaching arrangements of a particular kind we may have is purely a matter of expediency. We don't have vacation Bible schools from the moment school gets out until school takes back in, but VBS is a very effective teaching format. We don't have gospel meetings 52 weeks out of the year, but they are a very effective teaching format. I don't see how the problem you posed (having a constant round of funerals and weddings in the building) could ever be a practical reality because most people in any given community do not want the sound, solid, scriptural preaching which faithful brethren do at every opportunity.

Like yourself, I have no interest in pressing my views on things which ought to be left to the individual conscience and to each church. The young man who wrote and asked the question was motivated by a visiting preacher who spoke and who made it his business to preach a scathing condemnation of funerals and weddings in the building. The young man wanted to hear "the rest of the story," i.e., the arguments on the other side of the coin. If you will scan my letter again, you will see I avoided making any harsh comments at all about the offending speaker. I limited myself to the issue itself because I am not interested in seeing brethren cross swords on such matters. We have far more serious and pressing matters before us and we need to avoid being diverted from them. I know you share that goal. Those who read our brief exchange of views should realize that that is all it is: an exchange of views by two brethren who share a mutual love and respect. I know the two of us are not going to cause any disruption over this subject, and I hope others who read our brief exchange of views will keep it in that context. False teachers and those who compromise with them might like to see such disruption among faithful brethren, so as to divert attention from the real error and digression developing among us, but they will be sorely disappointed.

May God bless and keep you always.
In Christian love,
Ron

Funerals

Irven Lee

When I write or speak in an effort to teach I am doing so as an uninspired teacher. I do recognize the Bible as the revealed word of God. We should live in harmony with its teaching, and our practice should also conform to the divine pattern. Someone has well said that it is human to err. We should all continue to learn and to adjust our course or direction as we may discover a need to change.

In the earlier decades of my efforts as a preacher there were requests for dozens of funeral sermons. Almost every one of these was conducted in a house where people met for worship on the first day of the week. My brethren generally did the same. It seems that practically all considered that a place of worship was the proper place for the sad assembly. Even people who never obeyed the gospel or worshipped God were carried to the meeting house for these last hours with the bodies. If a man would not go there when he was well, it does seem strange to take him when he cannot help himself, but that was the custom.

Divided families often allowed the different parts of the family to select "their preacher" for some part in the funeral. Some of the funerals were conducted in meeting houses that belonged to one denomination or another. Each of us was told his part. Each then complied with the request. I have been in situations where I was not very welcome or comfortable. You readers were needed to tell me what to do. In such circumstances I did not try to preach a "protestant" sermon, but rather a gospel sermon. A Methodist preacher, a Presbyterian preacher, and I rode from a funeral to the cemetery and back together on one occasion that I well remember. We debated as we rode. Respect for the silence of the Scriptures and the instrument of music in worship were topics of discussion. Our joint participation that day was a little disjointed.

During these early decades of my preaching, the preacher was often requested to get singers for the funeral. On other occasions the family would arrange for some singers. Congregational singing was not the custom. Please understand that this is not written to show how it should be done now, but this is more like a confession. Custom is not the same as law, but it often makes the rules.

Over the years my part has usually been that of a follower rather than a leader in the matter of memorial services. The claim can be made that I have tried to preach truth to the living. Some things I would like to change, but the past does not change very easily. It just stubbornly stares at you as it was.

The heartbreaking digression that came about twenty five years ago grew out of a failure on the part of many of us who preached to be as vigilant as we should have been. We preached truth that we recognized as needed, but we did not realize the very great need to warn against the social gospel and institutionalism. The day came when many would not endure sound doctrine. When the voices of innovation began to be heard many of us were awakened by a sort of sudden shock. There began to be more of a questioning and examining of all doctrines and customs. There had been too much drifting. Since that shocking awakening there has been a certain amount of radicalism or extremism. There is need at this time for patience, love, and diligent study. In trying to get back to the old Jerusalem gospel, it is possible for us to run past Jerusalem on down to Jericho!

We are to walk by faith and not by sight (2 Cor. 5:7). We are not to shun or omit any of the counsel of God (Acts 20:26, 27). There is a passage to the living concerning their loved ones who had died in the faith (1 Thess. 4:13-18). This passage closes with the charge that we "comfort one another with these words." It is not a sin to preach on this text in the presence of the body of a friend who has died or on any other occasion. It is never out of season to preach the counsel or wisdom of God.

Those who object to funerals in buildings belonging to the church are taking some authority to themselves that I do not understand. Reading the Scriptures, praying together, and preaching truth that is clearly taught in the Bible is not a purely social function any more than a sermon on baptism in the same building on another occasion would be an unscriptural social affair. The special need for comforting words would not make the occasion sinful. There is no example of a funeral sermon in a building belonging to the church nor is there an example of a sermon on baptism in such a building. There is no example of a building which the church owned. Please remember that an approved example is not the only way the Lord has of teaching.

Funeral homes now provide chapels, and more and more funerals are conducted there. There is nothing wrong with this. Congregational singing is becoming more common. This, too, is safe, and I am glad to accept it. My argument in favor of using the meeting house for funerals is that the reading, praying, preaching, and singing are the same as at regularly scheduled services. This type service is safe, and I would like to encouarge it. Now that funerals are more often conducted in chapels provided by the undertakers the singing is often omitted. For those who prefer this, there can be nothing wrong with this arrangement. We are given no instructions to guide us in any sort of service in memory of the dead.

Use of the Church Building

Herschel Patton

Brethren who feel that it is the mission of the church to relieve the whole world and to provide social benefits in the form of banqueting and recreation have often charged those of us who object with believing the church building is sacred. They have said, "If an accident happened in front of the church building, you would let an injured person die because the church phone couldn't be used for calling an ambulance, water for relief provided, or the building for shelter from the elements." Since the church pays the phone and water bill, they say, "If the church provided these, then the church is doing something that we say is not its mission."

This actually happened while I was preaching during 1973 with the Jordan Park congregation in Huntsville, Alabama, right in front of the Jordan Park church building—a three car accident. No one died, but a man was injured—severely cut. It was raining, and the church building (porch) was used for shelter. The phone in the church building was used for reporting the accident, and water from the church building was used for the bleeding man. Now, I preach, and the Jordan Park church believes that it is not the mission of the church to serve as a welfare agency for the world—that the church is not to support and provide that which is not its mission. So, did the Jordan Park church, in the above case, contribute to an unbeliever and use its facilities for an unauthorized thing?

Expediencies—Incidentals

This matter involves the using of an expediency. The church building is an expediency, authorized by the command to "assemble." Who has the right to make laws regarding an expediency—e.g. "It must be rented" "of brick"—"of wood"—"painted white"—"have a steeple," etc.? Here is a place where good judgment and charity must be employed, not a Scripture. To force on others an opinion, as if it were Scripture, to the disturbance of peace, would be sinful (Rom. 14:15).

Churches often use expediencies to expedite work, such as the church building, and then there are "incidental" uses of an expediency which do not involve the church in its mission.

The church parking lot is often used by people who live nearby, are visiting, have business at an adjoining place, but this is not in the purpose and plans of the church, and the church, having neither purposed nor planned this, is not engaged in providing parking for the general public. If the church purposed a parking lot for public parking, it would then become a function of the church—an unscriptural function.

I recently visited a neighboring congregation during a meeting, and during the prayer there was suddenly the strains of instrumental music flowing from the public address system (an expediency provided by the church for more effective teaching). The system was picking up signals from the local radio station. Was that church providing instrumental music with the service? Of course, the church was not providing that, though it owned and had installed the system bringing it in. There was no purpose and plans for this on the part of the church. It was just something incidental. Likewise, the Jordan Park church did not purpose its building, with the plumbing and phone, as a first aid station. These facilities were used for this, all right, on the occasion mentioned, and may, sometime, be so used again. But it was not a case of the church purposefully engaging in something that is not its mission.

I have preached in meetings where the brethren habitually had "dinner on the ground" on the beginning day of the meeting, and a few times, when it started raining, everyone went into the meeting house, turned some of the benches around, facing each other, spread the dinner and ate—in the dry. Was some scriptural precept violated? I think not. That church building and the benches were not purposed and planned by the church as a place of eating together, and the church was not providing for "eating together" as part of its program of work. Such action was nothing more than an incidental use of an expedient, not at all involving the mission and work of the church. This is all together different from a church purposing and providing proper facilities for banqueting, recreation, a kindergarten, or anything else not in the prescribed mission of the church.

Radicalism

Because liberal brethren who do purpose and provide things not in the divinely revealed mission of the church, in an effort to justify themselves, often point to some of these "incidentals" on our part, some brethren have backed into radicalism and absurdness with reference to the use of church buildings. Some are saying that church buildings cannot be used for a wedding, funeral, or even an announcement concerning some activity that is not a work of every New Testament church. I have already mentioned "incidental" uses of an expedient where churches are not the participant. Concerning weddings and funerals in the church building, I believe these can be justified either as the church using an expedient in its work or as incidentals not involving the work and mission of the church.

True, you do not read of weddings or funerals in church buildings in the New Testament. But teaching is one of the things to be done that involves "place." What would afford a more effective time for impressive teaching on the sacredness, sanctity, and permanency of marriage than a wedding? The "wedding" could serve as an object lesson, like the little child Jesus one time used to enforce his teaching on humility. And, when would more impressive teaching concerning the certainty of death, eternity, and the need for preparedness, be done than at a funeral? The church building is not expected to be a funeral parlor or wedding chapel, but for actions involving an assembly for teaching and edifying. The wedding or funeral is simply an occasion for teaching. The church may not be obligated to furnish you a place to get married in, but your marriage can be an instrument for some very effective teaching which should be the chief objective of those charged with using judgment about incidentals.

On the other hand, weddings and funerals may be looked upon as incidental uses of the church building, granted to others. The activity is purely a family affair—planned and arranged by them—apart from the church's program of work. The church would no more be involved in this than it would in secular education if the school building burned down and the elders granted permission for classes to be conducted in the church building for a temporary time, with the school paying for the utilities and incidentals used. Granting permission for such uses of the church building would involve discernment concerning who, what, and how.

The church is not engaged in the work of social and secular activities when announcements are made about these things in the church building or church bulletin. The church building public address system, and bulletin are for teaching and edifying, which would involve teaching and admonishing people about important actions in their personal lives. If it is important for parents to "nurture" their children "in the Lord," it is proper for preachers, elders, or teachers to tell them so, warning of the dangers of infidelity and immorality in schools of learning and even identifying and recommending places where these dangers are at a minimum.

If the Bible teaches that Christians should seek out, and provide for their children wholesome social and recreational activities, it is proper for spiritual teachers to announce, identify, and encourage such, even in the church building while the saints are assembled. The church is neither contributing to nor furnishing secular education, or social endeavors, when parents are instructed and informed of where and how they may discharge their duties in this realm. In fact, there is Bible precedent for using the time and place of assembly for informing saints of personal duties. Paul wrote letters to the Colossians and Laodiceans and said for the letters to be read at each place and then exchange the letters and read (Col. 4:16), which letters contained numerous instructions to be followed by various individuals in their personal activities. For instance, the Colossian church was not contributing to or doing the work of masters when these were instructed, at the reading of Paul's letter, to "give unto your servants that which is just and equal" (Col. 4:1).

Instruction may be given saints at the church building, or in church bulletins, about Catholic aims and the dangers of one with these aims standing in the room of highest authority in the land, as was often done a few years back during an election campaign, but this is not comparable to the church building being used as a campaign headquarters. This would be putting the church, with its building, into the work of conducting an election campaign, which is not its mission.

A church is not making a contribution to, or helping do the work of a hospital or clinic when announcements are made in the church building about a need for blood donors and instruction about where and how to make the donation.

It is radicalism, indeed, for brethren to conclude that the church has engaged in something not its work when announcement and instruction are given in the church building, or bulletin, about an educational, medical, or social need wherein Christians have a responsibility, or to look upon some incidental action, not purposed or planned by the church, and say "the church has apostatized from its mission." It is good to carefully weigh all matters and always follow the prescribed path, but let us not try to make laws regarding expedients and incidentals and read into certain actions what is not there. Such action leads to strife and indicates we are the "nuts" that many charge us with being.

Guardian of Truth, XXVII: 13 (July 7, 1983), pp. 403-404

Regarding Weddings and Funerals in Meetinghouses

Bill Cavender

Some time ago a sincere brother wrote me regarding the scripturalness of having weddings and funerals in buildings owned by congregations. Here is the substance of, and quotations from my response:

As regarding the matter of which you wrote (a funeral in a meetinghouse, BC), I will not be able to give you an answer that will be altogether satisfactory. When matters of opinion and judgment become matters of faith and conscience with us and since there is nothing in God's will about such matters (except principles set forth in Romans 14 and 1 Corinthians 8-10), then no answer is satisfactory except one that agrees with our conviction. This is the great problem among conservative churches and brethren which is dividing us needlessly.

Under the guise of "standing for the truth" many conservative elders, preachers, and churches are dividing and sub-dividing. Most, if not all, of these divisions which are occurring over the country among so-called faithful churches (and within some of them where they are divided in sentiment but not physically) are over opinions. This is a tragic, terrible commentary on us. It is not the will of Christ. We need to stop it. We need to stop preaching our opinions as if they were law and gospel, matters clearly and plainly revealed by Jesus and his inspired apostles. We would do well to be silent where they were silent, not ever binding as a matter of duty, salvation, and truth that which they did not bind by revelation (Matt. 16:19; 18:18; John 16:13).

Meetinghouses are expedients. They are *generally* authorized because we are commanded to assemble, to worship, to study, to teach. To then begin to argue about every specific use of an expedient under all circumstances, the expedient uses of an expedient, is something the Bible does not talk about. To arrive at conclusions by devious processes of human reasonings ("if this is wrong, then this is then this is also wrong, *ad infinitum*; and "if this then is right, this is right," etc.) is not to walk by faith but by human reasonings and opinion. Expedient uses of church buildings and someone knowing *for sure* exactly what a building can be used for *under all circumstances* falls exactly into this category. This matter should not be (and should never be) an issue among brethren to argue about and be alienated over. Good, sound brethren will never agree on every facet of the matter for there is no Scripture bearing directly, specifically on such matters. Why make an opinion and judgment a matter of faith and conscience, a matter of diviseness and difference among brethren when it should not be so? Let every brother hold his own judgment in the matter, let the elders in each church decide this matter of judgment and opinion as they determine other such matters, and let us keep our opinions to ourselves.

Your comparison of this matter to "fellowship" parties and banquets and to the Herald of Truth is much like the "covering" brethren who tell me that a woman wearing a "covering" to worship is in the same category as the existence of God, the Deity of Jesus, and baptism for the remission of sins. They, like you, erroneously hold a matter of opinion as a matter of faith and conscience, confusing their categories. God has well spoken on the church, its organization and its work. The Herald of Truth is a doctrinal error and practice. The liberals' false use of the word "fellowship" in reference to eating and drinking, parties and recreation, is a doctrinal error. God has spoken on these matters. He has not spoken on the varied and expedient uses of expedients such as meetinghouses. Yet brethren almost always have the tendency, when they exalt a matter of opinion to a matter of faith and conscience, to place their convictions among the most important of doctrinal matters. Jews did this with their meats and days in Romans 14.

You should not hold this matter as one of faith, of conscience. That is your fundamental error. Out of this grows others: (1) You will find yourself at odds with faithful brethren who do not hold the same conviction, suspicions are aroused and feelings engendered, and little by little you will separate yourself from them and they from you. (2) Such matters make us appear ridiculous as a warring, factious, opinionated people in the eyes of an unbelieving, unconverted world. We have enough problems trying to convert a sinful, falsely-taught world to the plain truths of the gospel and about the church without, in effect, telling such people that they must also believe it sinful to have a funeral or wedding in a meetinghouse in order to serve Christ, do God's will, and go to heaven. (3) By holding such opinions as matters of faith, you will be compelled from time to time to refuse participation in weddings or funerals, your work will sooner or later be troublesome wherever you are, you will divide and alienate brethren (as some will always follow what a preacher believes) when you don't need to do so over such unimportant matters. I urge and exhort you to not feel so strongly about such matters, to be flexible, to hold this as opinion and not faith, and to graciously let others differ with you.

As a practical matter, this is a moot question and problem. What is so important about it? Our building here is ten years old and there has never been a funeral in it. It has been years since I've preached a funeral in a meetinghouse. I do not average one wedding a year in a meetinghouse. Most other preachers don't. Why on earth be so concerned about something that is hardly practiced and had never been, until recently, any kind of troublesome matter among us? When weddings and funerals in meetinghouses were much more common than now, no one ever raised a problem about, it. Now when it is hardly ever done, brethren are kicking about it and even dividing over it. Why? To me it is foolish and sinful for brethren to divide over non-essential matters.

I don't have all the answers to expedient uses of expedients. You don't either. That's why you ought not to feel too strongly about such matters. As far as I am personally concerned, I think some of the best lessons are taught at funerals and weddings. I see more seriousness, solemnity, and sincerity at funerals and weddings than upon some other occasions. Such are excellent opportunities to preach the gospel, in a meetinghouse or anywhere else. My judgment is that we can and should do so if someone wants to have a funeral or wedding in a meetinghouse. My preference is that funerals be at funeral homes and weddings be in family homes. But I will not make my judgments and preferences matters of faith and conscience, and will not try to let my conscience be the guide for someone else's conscience. I don't think you should either. This is about all I know in this matter. I trust these thoughts will be helpful.

Weddings and Funerals in the Meetinghouse (1)

Weldon E. Warnock

A feeling has arisen in the minds of some good brethren that the meetinghouse may not be used for weddings or funerals. They are saying that the church building was erected with the Lord's money, and, therefore, it may only be used for authorized church functions. This position, as I see it, is an extreme and inconsistent one.

It is granted that the Lord's money when used in building construction should only be used to erect facilities that expedite the church's authorized work. The church has no right to build kitchens and dining halls for social purposes, wedding chapels, or funeral parlors. These things do not constitute the work of the church. But for the building to be used for a wedding or funeral is something else. No divine principle is violated in any way by such usage of the building. Really, the Lord never did say what could or could not be done in a meeting house. He informed the church how to conduct itself, but said nothing about the meeting house. Hence, the issue is a matter of judgment and expediency. However, in the exercise of this liberty, nothing should be done that is in poor taste or that reflects upon the cause of Christ.

Brethren talk about the meetinghouse not being holy,

then turn around and treat it like Solomon's temple. Some chide the too liberal brethren for their "dedication service" of the new church building. Right here is where the matter becomes rather ironic. The too liberal brethren "dedicate" their building to the Lord and then make a big ado about it not being sacred. Whereas some of the "conservative" brethren would have nothing to do with a "dedicatorial service" but act toward the building as though it was a sacred shrine on holy ground. I see a little taint of the Catholic attitude in this concept of the meetinghouse.

If no weddings or funerals may be conducted in the building because they are not functions of the church, then we are going to have to quit socializing before and after worship. Everything in the world (an exaggeration, wew) is discussed by the brethren in the building—from little junior's cutting of teeth to the number of coons old Blue treed the night before. These things must come to a halt if consistency is to be attained. There can be no conversation, other than on the Bible until you get off church property. After all, the church's money was not spent to provide a place to discuss coon hunting.

Too, I am certain that the church's yard and parking area bear the same relationship to this problem as the meetinghouse does. I do not think that one can logically say that the building should be anymore restricted than the outside premises. Both were bought with the same money. Hence, if the meetinghouse may not be used for anything other than church functions, then neither may the outside grounds. We are therefore forced to enclose the premises with a fence to prohibit football games, hopscotch, tag, etc. by the neighborhood children. Fencing the lot will also prevent the townspeople, in some places, parking on the property during the week while they shop or work.

Remember that the parking lot was not built for a neighborhood playground or a public parking lot. If the meetinghouse may not be used for weddings and funerals because it was not built for these purposes, then neither may the parking lot be used for games and public parking because it was not built for these purposes. If some brethren's thinking is sound on the meeting house, the same kind of thinking is valid on the parking lot. If not, why not?

But someone says, "The public will get the wrong impression of the church if weddings and funerals are permitted." Here is where teaching enters the picture. We must teach the public. Really, I do not know of any that has gotten harmful impressions from a wedding or funeral in the building. There are some that are getting distorted concepts and impressions of extremism from those who refuse to allow them in the building. One woman said, when her daughter, who had recently become a Christian, was not allowed to have her wedding in the building, "She was refused because she did not grow up in that church."

Our children attend the services of the church all of their young lives, then when they get ready to marry, they are forced to go to another congregation's building where weddings are not objectionable. Oh yes, the opposition to weddings in a church building (at the home congregation, anyway) are right there to watch and give their blessings to the couple. Inconsistent, would not you say?

It seems to me that instead of getting so stringent on weddings and funerals in the meetinghouse, there needs to be a lot of emphasis on the non-use of the building. Brethren will spend from 100 to 200 thousand dollars on a structure, then use it about four hours a week. A good portion of the weekly contribution is consumed paying on the debt for fifteen to twenty years, just to have a place to meet a few hours each week. This non-use does not seem to bother some of the brethren, but mention a wedding and they quickly respond about the misuse of the building. Let's make the meetinghouse a center for special classes, training and development, and a host of other work that comes within the church's mission. We need to be better stewards of church property.

Weddings and Funerals (1)
(A Review)

Ralph D. Williams

Brother Weldon Warnock raised some good questions in his article, "Weddings and Funerals in the Meeting house" in the February 1973 issue. It seems more brethren are becoming concerned over these practices lately. *Searching the Scriptures* is to be commended for allowing the question to be searched openly.

It appears that three basic questions need to be considered as a solution is sought: (1) Are these activities a work of the local church? (2) Can church facilities be used for an individual/family need in providing for a social/domestic affair (1 Tim. 5:8)? (Though the state of marriage is ordained of God how it is entered is not). (3) Can the church facilities be used by a citizen to comply with his civil obligations? A marriage ceremony (of some kind not necessarily religious) is required by civil law.

The real issue is: where is the authority? If such practices are allowable a simple N.T. precept, example or necessary inference is all that's necessary. Positive authority is needed, not a negative "what does it violate" approach ("where does the Bible say not to play?"). Because brethren may like it, young people expect it, and churches "traditionally" practice it, doesn't make it right.

In his second and last paragraphs, Brother Warnock recognizes that the church has an "authorized work" to do, and admits the building expedites such. Surely none can challenge that principle. Then it simply remains to determine what the "authorized work" is and use the facilities accordingly.

I would take exception to the statement, "The Lord never did say what could or could not be done in a meetinghouse." Jesus told us that when he revealed the "church's authorized work." Don't forget it's the work of the church that necessarily infers authority for a building to begin with! If the collectivist did not have a work to do requiring a meeting place, no reason nor right would exist for such a place. Thus the "work" and the "place" to do that work go together. Therefore the "place" exists for only one exclusive purpose—to "expedite the church's authorized work."

To speak of brethren having a "taint of Catholic attitude" in acting as though the building were "a sacred shrine on holy ground" is prejudicial and serves no purpose in clarifying the issue. All will agree the meeting place is not sacred as was Solomon's temple. But still there is a principle of "sanctification" (a setting apart) involved. Is the Lord's treasury not "set apart" to be used as he wills? Likewise are not those items purchased with those Divine funds "set apart" for the special use as the N.T. directs? Is it possible to be guilty of profaning such items by using them in a "common way" (Heb. 12:16)?

To compare weddings with "socializing" before and after services isn't parallel. If a special social hour were scheduled and all invited to come for that purpose we'd be comparing things of like nature. This argument is somewhat like the liberals reply, "you have a water fountain in the building," when we object to their kitchens and dining rooms. If a "socializing meeting were called, brother Warnock would have a parallel argument; just as our liberal kitchen-banqueting brethren would have, if we were to announce a special meeting around the water cooler. But in both cases we're talking about individual doings which are incidental in using the building.

As brethren assemble, greetings are proper, comments beyond that which is spiritually edifying would be a matter for the individual to regulate. Personally I try to refrain from secular socializing, and keep in mind the purpose for which we've assembled. Granted this isn't always easy. If this area needs more emphasis we should attend to it. But the point is a special service hasn't been called for "social visiting" as for a wedding.

I don't know of any churches or elders inviting the public to freely use the parking lot for the neighborhood children to turn the premises into a play lot. If someone came to the elders requesting such use, they ought to explain the lot wasn't designed for such purposes and suggest the inquirer look elsewhere. If a brother requested his family use the parking lot for games to facilitate his son's birthday party, I believe that would be more parallel to requesting use of the church building for a wedding. Wouldn't we expect the elders to deny such a request?

Of course how these questions are answered regarding socializing and using the parking lot doesn't really meet the issue of using the building for weddings and funerals. First tackle this primary issue itself. Then if these other matters need attention for consistency and truth's sake, work at solving them. But keep in mind the right or wrong of "weddings" in the meetinghouse isn't answered by what incidentally takes place by non-members on the parking lot.

Liberal brethren have argued to justify their secular schools and kindergartens in the building on the grounds that it stands idle so many hours each week. Our failure to utilize the facilities more fully doesn't scripturally justify opening the door for unauthorized works. I agree we should use the building more for "special classes . . . (etc.) *that comes within the church's mission"* (emphasis mine, RW). Brother Warnock's concluding words, as his beginning (second) paragraph, knocks weddings and funerals out of the building—unless scriptural proof can be given that such are within the church's mission.

Weddings and Funerals in the Meetinghouse (2)

Weldon E. Warnock

Brother Ralph Williams said in a review of my February article on "Weddings and Funerals in the Meetinghouse" that "The real issue is: Where Is the Authority? If such practices are allowable a simple N.T. precept, example or necessary inference is all that's necessary." But the issue is not one of authority (finding book, chapter, and verse), but rather it is a matter of judgment. We are not talking about what the church may do, but what individuals may do in the meetinghouse. Certainly the church has no business conducting weddings or funerals in or out of the meetinghouse. We are all in agreement here. But what individuals may do in the church's building is another matter.

To ask for book, chapter and verse for a wedding or funeral in the meetinghouse is about like asking for Bible to comb your hair, tie your shoes, powder your face, or manicure your nails in the meetinghouse. Where is the command, example, or necessary inference for these things in the meetinghouse? Yet, we all do them (hopefully, not during the worship, however). The church would need authority to comb hair, tie shoes, powder the face, and manicure nails, but not individuals.

Our brother states, "I would take exception to the statement, 'The Lord never did say what could or could not be done in a meetinghouse.' Jesus told us that when he revealed the 'church's authorized work.'" No, brother Williams, Jesus told the church what it could do when he revealed its authorized work—not what could be done in a temporal structure. This position eliminates any and everything in the building or on the premises that is not a work of the church. Is riding a bicycle on the parking lot a work of the church? Is playing ball by the neighborhood children a work of the church? Is public parking by the community while shopping or working the church's work? Since none of these things is a work of the church, they must be barred from church property, according to brother Williams' reasoning.

Forced to its logical conclusion, brother Williams' view becomes an extreme and untenable one. It could be classified as a *reductio ad absurdum*. Putting this in plain language, it means, "disproof of a proposition, etc., by showing the absurdity to which it leads when carried to its logical conclusion" (Webster). Brother Williams' position demands that everything not related to church activity must be kept off the church's premises. No congregation practices this.

My comparison of weddings and funerals to socializing before and after services is parallel, brother Williams to the contrary. I did not say that they were comparable in every aspect, but they are parallel in that neither is a function of the church. Since some are contending that weddings and funerals may not be conducted in a meetinghouse because they are not works of the church, I maintained in my former article that neither may socializing, games by neighborhood children or parking of automobiles by the local residents while shopping or working, be done on the church's premises because they are not functions of the church.

Brother Williams wants to make the socializing proper and permissible before and after worship on the basis of it being incidental. Webster defines "incidental" as "a chance or undesigned feature of something; casual; hence, minor; of secondary importance." Thus, it appears that brother Williams has no objections to undesigned secular matters in the meetinghouse; just those that are planned. Maybe we need to start having unplanned weddings and classify them under "incidentals." To say a thing is incidental seems to make it right. Seriously, we have as much right to perform a wedding or funeral in the meetinghouse and classify it a matter of judgment as we do to talk about hunting there and classify it an incidental. Neither one involves the church in an unauthorized practice.

Our brother said, "I don't know of any churches or elders inviting the public to freely use the parking lot or the neighborhood children to turn the premises into a play lot." Why don't they stop the practice, then? If their failure to invite suggests that they disapprove, then they ought to terminate playing and parking on the premises. The fact that elders do not stop playing and public parking on the parking lot is evidence that they have no objections. How many churches do you think would turn down children's request to ride their bicycles on the parking lot or deny a request for some business people to use the lot while they are at work? To be this narrow and restrictive would cast the church in a contemptible position in the community.

Who says that weddings and funerals are the primary issue, except brethren who have made them an issue?

They are no issue with most of us, and I regret that they have been made a public issue. If I made children playing on the parking lot and socializing before and after worship an issue, they would be the main issue with me. I could say something like brother Williams said, "Of course how these questions are answered regarding weddings and funerals doesn't really meet the issue of using the church's premises for children playing and public parking. First tackle the primary issue itself. Then if these other matters need attention for consistency and truth's sake, work at solving them." Really, public parking and playing on the parking lot are just as much an issue as weddings and funerals in the building, and "for consistency and truth's sake," they need solving by the objectors of weddings and funerals in the building.

Some questions are in order just here: (1) Since brother Williams contended that the church's facilities are "sanctified," would it be permissible for a person to make a phone call on the church's phone that is not related to church work? (2) Could a person get a drink of water when the church is not assembled in the building? (3) May the restrooms be used, other than during a service? These things are done in all buildings owned by churches of Christ that are so equipped. Are we to quit allowing these practices on the basis of the facilities being "sanctified"—that they are to be used only in conjunction with the church's activity?

Although I am of the conviction that the usage of the building for weddings and funerals is a matter of judgment, there are some factors to consider as to what may be permitted on the church's premises: (1) Is it morally right? Of course, this goes without saying. (2) What might the potential dangers be to involving the church in the practice later? (3) Would the people in the community get the wrong impression and thus hinder them from obeying the truth? (4) Has the main purpose of the meeting house been changed? It was built for the worship and work of the church. If it is used all week for individual projects and activities, has not the purpose for which it was built been altered? As the old saying goes, "The tail would be wagging the dog." (5) Is the activity in good taste? Propriety demands, on the basis of the close proximity of the meeting house with religious functions, that certain things are out of place on the church's property. Discretion would have to be used here.

In conclusion may I say that, if a congregation saw fit to refuse a wedding or funeral in its meetinghouse, that would be its prerogative, but it has no right to try to impose its opinions or feelings on sister congregations and thereby disrupt the peace and harmony of brethren over such matters that are purely optional. We have enough legitimate issues without creating some superfluous ones.

Weddings and Funerals (Review 2)

Ralph D. Williams

Brother Weldon Warnock and I agree the church is not in the business of providing for weddings and funerals. I'm sure we'd agree that such is an individual and family responsibility (1 Cor. 7:2; 1 Tim. 5:8). Yet, when the meetinghouse is used for these affairs, who has provided the place? The individual didn't spend his money to build the facilities. The building, seating, etc. were purchased from the Lord's (church) treasury. If a church were renting a meeting place would it be all right to use church funds to rent it an extra hour or another evening for a wedding?

Combing the hair and clipping a hangnail, like using the restroom or drinking fountain, need no specific authority. These are individual personal needs which are merely incidental to the reason for being at the building. To have a parallel with a wedding one would need to announce that brethren were invited to gather with combs and clippers at a certain time for a special service of clipping and combing.

I'll stand upon my statement that Jesus told us how to use the meeting house when he revealed the "church's authorized work." Obviously the Lord said nothing concerning "a temporal structure" *per se*. Yet places of assembling are recorded in the N.T. (Acts 20:8,10). And the work and worship required of the church necessitate a place (1 Cor. 11:18-22; Heb. 10:25). Therefore when a place is rented or purchased with the Lord's funds to do his authorized work, the question of how to use the place should be self-evident!

How shall we use the communion trays? Some seem uncertain about the building itself, but what about this aid to the Lord's supper? Would a sister decide to take the bread plates home to serve sandwiches at a bridal shower since the trays weren't being used anyway? The reasoning of some would permit it. The question then is will we use an expedient (building, trays, baptistry) only for the use for which it was purchased with the Lord's funds? In the business world one who takes company property for his own personal use without authority is guilty of misappropriation. We don't wish to spiritually misappropriate the Lord's funds or property. That's the very heart of this discussion.

Brother Warnock calls my view absurd because he carries it out to an "extreme and untenable" conclusion, which he thinks is necessary. He says no congregation practices keeping off the church's premises everything not related to church activity. (Is our standard of right and wrong to be what churches practice?) Certainly we can't police the grounds or put up barbed wire to stop children from riding their bicycles or playing on it. But the fact remains the parking lot wasn't built as a playground. Neither was it designed to aid shoppers and business men. Such uses are incidental. If it's a problem put up a sign: "church parking." That states the purpose of this private property. If people violate it, we can't control that nor would it be wise to make a scene over it. Because we can't completely control what outsiders do on the premises doesn't argue or justify planning and using church facilities in nearly anyway anyone may desire.

True, socializing before and after services is parallel to weddings in that neither are the function of the church. But they are not parallel where it would be significant in this discussion. "Socializing" or visiting is not a planned activity. Time is not set apart for it. Announcements and invitations are not extended for participation. A special service is not scheduled for that purpose. A request is not made of the elders that the building might be borrowed for such use. I've never heard an outsider speak of our "visiting" as they've been heard to speak about a "church of Christ wedding."

The careful attention given the word "incidental" is important and appreciated. It means "a chance or undesigned feature of something; casual; hence, minor; of secondary importance." Surely this is part of the key in resolving some of the seeming difficulties in this inquiry. "Incidentals" are a fact of life; something we must live with. They are even found in the Bible. For example, in connection with baptism, who administered it and where were merely incidentals (1 Cor. 1:17; Acts 8:36). However, it's a little hard to believe many brides would be satisfied with an "unplanned" (incidental) wedding. While "socializing" may be "incidental" much of that which I hear is an expression of "care one for another" (1 Cor. 12:25) and courtesy toward visitors (Gal. 6:10). The content of such visiting is indeed a matter of judgment. But this is not the same and I would object if the men wished to meet at the building one evening to talk about and show slides of a hunting trip.

Is it wrong to use the facilities purchased with the Lord's money only for those things for which they were needed in the first place? Should the wishes of the public determine their use? I don't find it narrow to kindly and politely tell folks that the church premises aren't designed for general public use. Tell them (with a smile) if they want to park there to come Sunday at 9 a.m.! Right thinking people, respectful of private property, shouldn't become offended at this truth. Of course the first consideration ought always to be whether our practice and attitude is offensive to God.

Again, if the word "sanctified" causes misunderstanding, substitute the words "ear-marked" or "reserved" with regard to the use of the facilities. Clearly none believe the building is like some shrine in which we must remain silent or whisper in hushed tones. The meeting place is "set apart" for the special work of the Lord. The worship that is rendered therein is truly "sanctified" in the strictest biblical sense of the word.

In response to the three questions: the telephone, like the restroom, exists not specifically for "church work" but to facilitate those who assemble or are at the building at other times (cleaning, bulletin, studying). It serves one's needs while there spiritually or secularly. I wouldn't object if one phoned to check with the baby sitter, called a taxi or ambulance, etc. I would oppose a member coming to the building solely to make social or business calls. If one were at the building legitimately, the use of the phone would be merely incidental. If a brother didn't have water or bathroom facilities at home, I'm sure he'd be welcome to come to the building at any hour there was need. In such trying circumstances he'd no doubt classify as a "needy saint" anyway, thus an object of church aid. But if one has utilities at home, why would he make a special trip to the meetinghouse? The telephone, water, restrooms all serve the incidental needs of those who have reason to be at the building, during services or any other time.

Again, brother Warnock and I agree when he writes in his next to the last paragraph, the meetinghouse "was built for the worship and work of the church." Is it improper or "absurd" to ask brethren simply to apply that truth in practice? The building wasn't built for public use by the Garden club, Rotary, 4H-club, Boy Scouts, *ad infinitum*. Therefore the list of five rules or someone else's ten rules aren't needed to determine what activities may be permitted on the premises and by whom. The church has a work and worship to attend to. A place was necessary to accomplish it. Therefore let us be content to use the facilities for which they were originally acquired and authorized.

While some may consider this a superfluous issue, others are concerned enough to investigate and discuss it calmly and brotherly in the interest of doing only what is right. Let us help ourselves and our brethren never to depreciate a question to the extent we fail to fulfil 1 Thessalonians 5:21.

www.ingramcontent.com/pod-product-compliance
Lightning Source LLC
Chambersburg PA
CBHW061155040426
42445CB00013B/1687